My FIRST HUNT!

Written by
Beverly King

Illustrated by
Navya

My dad woke me up early on Saturday morning and said, "**Hubba**, **Hubba**, rise and shine! Breakfast is on the table!" I smiled back at him, excited for the day ahead.

work
dream

Today is a special day.

A day I have been waiting for as long as I can remember. My dad and I are going deer hunting!

I put on my green and brown **camouflage** shirt and pants, along with my brown hiking boots. Then I grabbed my hunting hat as I headed to the kitchen for breakfast.

Angel

JAM

I have been wearing my hunting camos for years, but this year is different.

This year, I will be hunting with my dad, not just watching.

This year, I drew a whitetail doe tag along with my mom, while my dad drew a buck tag. My mom and dad filled their tags earlier in the week, and now it's time to fill my tag.

TAG-01.COM

DEER

TURKEY

BOBCAT

ELK

GUIDE
RULES & REGULATIONS

During the spring, I completed my hunter's safety course.

I learned how to be a **responsible** and **ethical** hunter and how to safely carry and shoot the rifle.

I have practiced shooting my rifle over the last few years and am eager to put it in action.

During breakfast, my dad said, "This will be a great day to hunt. The moon is full, and the wind has died down."

When breakfast was over, we loaded up the truck as the sun began to rise and headed out towards the mountains.

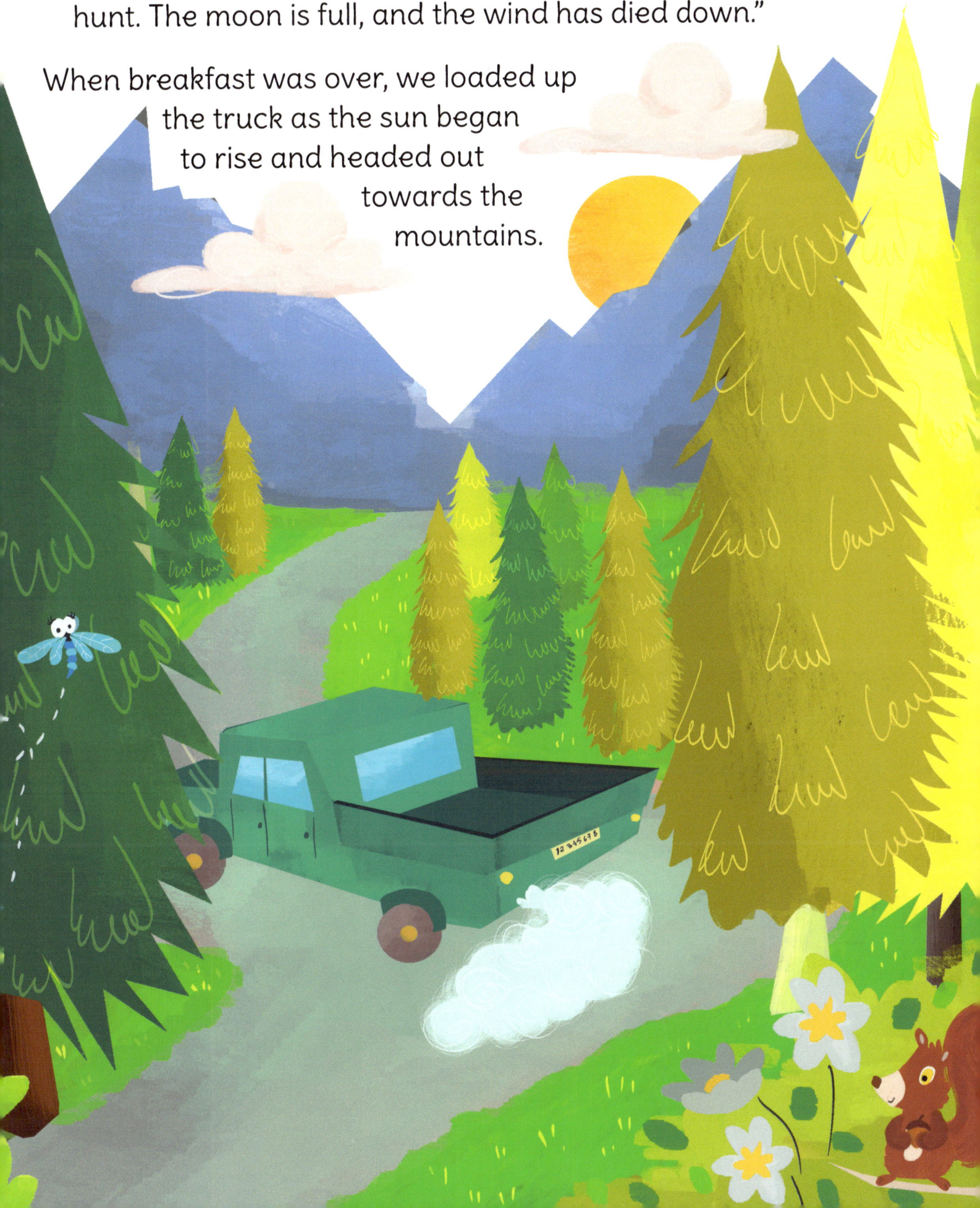

During the drive, my dad told me the story of his first hunt. His dad had a secret spot they would go to, and it would be just them with no one else around for miles.

I smiled and listened as my dad also smiled while talking about how much he learned about hunting from his parents and grandparents.

On my dad's first hunt, he didn't
get a deer. He had seen deer, but
he didn't have a clean shot. He reminded
me that a clean shot is a very important
requirement as we **never** want an animal to suffer.

A single, well-placed shot is required to ethically take home a
deer. They are beautiful animals that deserve our respect. My
dad didn't get a deer until his second time out hunting. He said
it was worth the wait.

I wondered how my first
hunting story would go.

Once we arrived at the hunting area, we unloaded the truck, grabbed the big game cart with our hunting packs, and picked up our guns, making sure the ammunition was secure and the safety was on. We walked through the quaking aspen, Douglas firs, and lodgepole pine trees, and over the rolling hills.

Along the way, up in the trees, we saw American robins, gray jays, and some mountain quail. There were even red squirrels running along the tree branches.

On the ground, we saw black-tailed jackrabbits and ruffed grouse running about.

Up on the far ridge, we spotted a bobcat and even a black bear off in the distance. Circling in the sky were a few bald eagles along with red-tailed hawks as they searched the area looking for food.

We walked as quietly as we could so as not to scare the animals.

When we arrived at an open spot, we put down our gear. My dad and I looked through our binoculars, scanning the area for deer.

We sat for several minutes, which seemed like hours to me, until my dad spotted the perfect white-tailed deer. He showed her to me and asked if I was ready. I nodded and said yes with excitement and fear, thinking this was my chance to finally shoot a deer.

I took a deep breath as I looked through my scope.

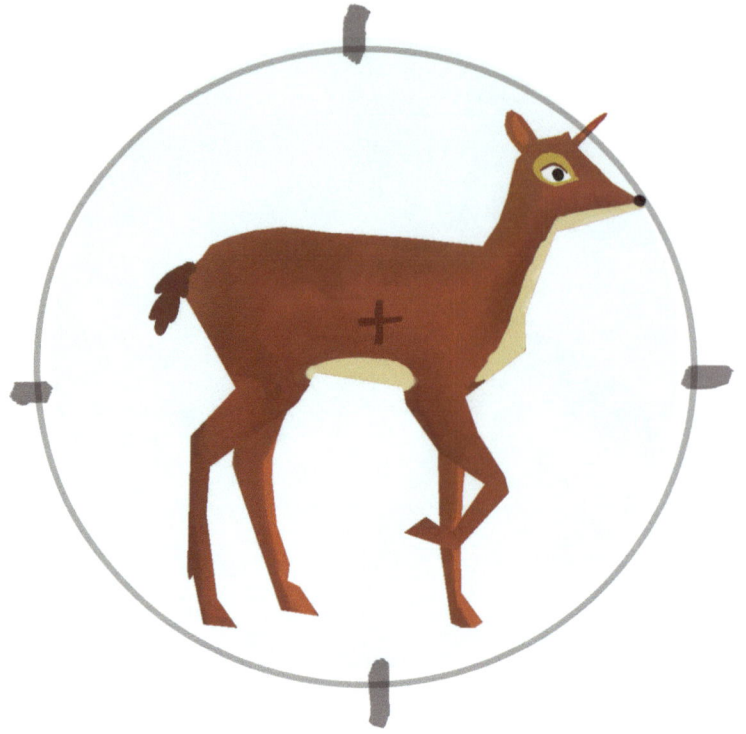

Then I took off the safety as my dad checked my aim. He said, "Shoot when you're ready." I squeezed the trigger as my heart raced inside my chest.

My dad yelled, "You got her!" I was so excited that I screamed. I safely put down my gun, and gave my dad a high five and a great **big hug**.

We walked over to the deer, and I started to cry. It was at that moment I realized I had killed a real deer, and my heart sank with sadness.

My dad reminded me why we hunt. We hunt to put food on the table and to keep the herds healthy.

He reminded me that without hunters, the herds can get overpopulated. Then the ecosystem would become out of balance and the deer could get sick, and they would suffer. We bowed our heads and gave our thanks.

Then my dad told me something unexpected and amazing. This was the very ridge that my grandfather took him on for his first hunt. Now it's part of my story.

We loaded the deer onto the game cart, placed a tarp to cover the deer, and pulled it back through the trees and over the rolling hills back to the truck.

Once we were back at the truck, we loaded the deer up along with the gear. My dad called my mom and gave her the news.
Then we headed **back home** as the sun began to set.

Once we were back home, we unloaded the truck and hung the deer in the garage.

We packed ice inside the deer so the deer would not spoil. Then we washed up and got ready for dinner.

Over dinner, my mom asked me how my day was. I smiled proudly as I told my mom about where we went and what we saw. I talked about all the excitement that had gone through my mind as my dad helped me take the perfect shot. My parents smiled as they listened to me talk about our day while I shared my first hunting **story**.

Glossary

Quaking aspen:

A North American deciduous tree that is fast-growing and can reach up to 65 to 80 feet at maturity. They are well known for their color-changing leaves in the fall.

Douglas fir:

This tree is the largest and tallest member of the pine family. They are medium-sized to extremely large trees that can grow from 70 to 330 feet tall and up to 8 feet in diameter. They also have a life span of up to 1,400 years.

Lodgepole pine:

A tall, slender, straight tree growing from 130 to 160 feet and can live up to 140 years. Lodgepole pines are one of the first trees to invade after a wildfire. Their cones are protected by a seal of pitch that requires fire or heat to release the seeds. This allows the seeds to stay on the tree or on the ground for many years until disturbance provides suitable growing conditions.

Bald eagle:

The bald eagle is the only eagle unique to North America. The bald eagle's scientific name signifies a sea eagle with a white head. The word "bald" at one time meant "white," not hairless. Bald eagles are found throughout most of North America from Alaska and Canada to Mexico. Half of the world's largest population of bald eagles live in Alaska. Male and female adult birds have a blackish-brown back and breast with a white head, neck, and tail along with yellow feet and legs, and pale, yellow eyes.

American robins:

The American robin is a migratory songbird. They are widely distributed throughout North America. The American robin has a brown back and a reddish-orange breast, varying from rich red maroon to peachy orange. The sexes are similar, but the female tends to be duller than the male, with a brown tint to the head, brown upperparts, and less bright underparts.

Black bear:

Adult males typically weigh between 126 to 551 pounds, while females weigh from 90 to 375 pounds. The American black bear can be distinguished from those of the Asian black bears by the lack of a white blaze on the chest and hairier footpads. Despite their name, American black bears show a great deal of color variation. The individual coat colors can range from white, blonde, cinnamon, light brown, or dark chocolate brown to jet black, with many intermediate varieties existing. Their keenest sense is their sense of smell, which is about seven times more sensitive than a domestic dog. They are excellent and strong swimmers. Their life span is anywhere from 18 - 39 years in the wild.

Red squirrels:

The red squirrels are primarily herbivores rodents. They have a typical head-to-body length of 7.5 to 9 inches with a tail length of 6 to 8 inches. Their tail helps them to balance and steer while jumping from tree to tree along with running along the tree branches. The red squirrel, like most tree squirrels, has sharp, curved claws to help them climb and descend tree trunks, thin branches, and even house walls. Their strong hind legs enable them to leap between trees and swim.

Redtail hawk:

Male red-tailed hawks may weigh between 1.52 to 2.87 pounds and females may weigh between 1.76 to 3.79 pounds. Male red-tailed hawks can measure 18 to 24 inches in total length where females measure 19 to 26 inches long. Their wingspan typically can range from 3 to 4 feet wide. Their most common prey are small rodents such as the mouse. They have been known to also consume other birds, reptiles, and fish.

Gray Jay:

The gray jay is also known as the Canada jay, grey jay, camp robber, or whiskey jack. They are a large songbird that has a pale gray under part, a darker upper part, and a gray-white head. Typically, the adult birds are between 9.8 to 13.0 inches long with a wing-span around 18 inches. They weigh around 2.3 to 2.5 ounces with an average life of 8 years.

Mountain Quail:

The mountain quail is a small ground-dwelling bird. Their average length is 10 to 11 inches. They have relatively short rounded wings and long featherless legs. They are easily recognized by their top knots, which are shorter on the female. They have a brown face, gray breast, brown back, and a heavily white underside.

Black-tailed jackrabbit:

The black-tailed jackrabbit is one of the largest North American hares. The young are born fully furred with eyes open. They are well-camouflaged and are mobile within minutes of birth. Female black-tailed jackrabbits do not protect or even stay with their young except during nursing. Their diets are composed of various shrubs, small trees, and grasses. The black-tailed jackrabbit is an important prey species for many raptors and carnivores such as eagles, hawks, owls, coyotes, and foxes.

Ruffed grouse:

These chunky, medium-sized birds weigh from 0.99 to 1.65 pounds and measure from 16 to 20 inches across with their short, strong wings. Both genders are similarly marked and sized, making them difficult to tell apart. The female often has a single white dot on their tail feathers and the males often have more than one white dot.

Bobcat:

The bobcat is a medium-sized cat native to North America. It has distinctive black bars on its forelegs and a black-tipped, stubby, or bobbed tail, from which they get their name. Though the bobcat prefers rabbits, it hunts insects, chicken, geese, and other birds, small rodents, and deer. Prey selection depends on their location and habitat, season, and abundance.

Questions

1. Why is hunting important?

2. What does it take to be a good hunter?

3. Where should you aim your gun?

4. Why do they have different hunting seasons?

5. Do different states have different rules and regulations?

6. What does hunting mean to you?

Dedicated to

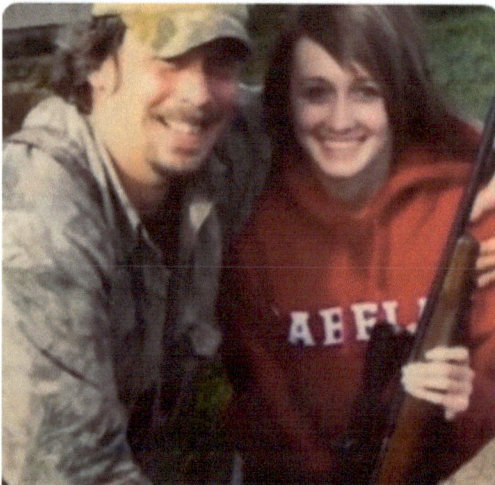

Dedicated to my mom for always believing in me, my dad for teaching me valuable lessons, my husband for continuing the tradition, and to my daughter for always wanting to learn. Special thanks to my sister Kimberly, my friend Joanna Forlino-Tjaden, and family members Cindy, Kathy, and Valerie for their support along the way.

beverlyschildrensbooks@gmail.com

www.ingramcontent.com/pod-product-compliance
Lightning Source LLC
Chambersburg PA
CBHW042019090426
42811CB00015B/1684